The Life and Times of Frank Balistrieri:

The Last, Most Powerful Godfather of Milwaukee

By

Wayne Clingman and Zack Long

Table of Contents

Dedication

To Barbara: qui sciebant?

<u>Forward</u>

Christian Cipollini

*Organized Crime Historian * True Crime Author * Comic Book Creator*

Sex, drugs, booze, bets and blood... the long and sordid history of America's love/hate affair with organized crime is rife with everything vice and violent. Is it the decadence that piques our interest? To observe, study or even live vicariously through the outlaw rebellion? Or is the magnetic draw of the criminal underworld simply the result of we humans trying to find the humanity within a sector of society that appears so outrageously inhumane… to understand or possibly relate to those who appear (on the surface) as completely antisocial or outright sociopathic? Perhaps the answer is a combination of all the aforementioned, or perhaps it's none of the above! Regardless of the where and why of our fascination with true crime, and in this case, organized crime, originates - one common denominator, a thread that's been woven into our culture since at least the time of Prohibition, remains strong - our insatiable hunger for more!

From books to movies to podcasts, spanning the field of biographical to the entirely fictionalized, we can't get enough of crime stories, legends, mysteries, dramas, and documentaries. And that's not a bad thing. For one, it keeps those of us who research and write about this stuff very busy and I thank you!). More importantly though - the interest in crime history, the enigmatic protagonists known as gangsters' (not to mention the wildly hedonistic lifestyles they are perceived to indulge in) is as relevant today as it was a century ago. Why? The Mob still exists (albeit in a drastically different fashion than during its heyday), the 'war on drugs' - a fight that began long before the creation of the DEA, I assure you - still rages on, and organized crime is that singular, elusive creature that penetrated nearly every sector of society, pressed its fangs into everything from the economy to popular culture and even into our combined subconscious. A phenomenon that basically established itself as a parallel of legit society, yet crosses the lines that theoretically never intersect (not even mathematical rules apply, they're outlaws ya know!) And essentially created a symbiotic relationship where the upper and under-worlds became dependent on one another, for better or worse.

When the collective psyche of our pop culture obsessed media visualizes the words like 'mafia' and 'gangster' - often first comes images of the obvious and usual suspects:

Capone, Gotti, and Bugsy; Chicago, New York, Las Vegas. On the flip side however, the 'poster boys' of American Gangsterism represent just a portion of the vastly larger portrait and significance the 'Mob' has seared into the epidural layers of so-called legitimate society's facade for over a century. What's more, the infamy held by the most notorious of gangland bad boys has perhaps overshadowed an invaluable history of lesser-known geographic and demographic factions that served as vital parts of Mafia's infiltration into everyday life, in every corner of the country. Despite being some of the most mystifying, intriguing and pivotal figures, many of these characters and the legacies of contributions to the criminal archives are lesser known outside their own regions. That's where researchers like the author of this tale comes in to explore, unveil and in some cases - dismiss historical inaccuracies - ultimately shining a light on the significance not only in their corner of the world but across the entire malevolent underworld.

One such shadowy, (yet crucial) figure who managed to remain out of the greater public limelight (and probably preferred it that way) ruled Milwaukee's mob for an unprecedented length of time, held influence across crime families and vested interest in one of the biggest Las Vegas crime scams of the latter twentieth century. You're about to meet him and take a tour of the seedier side of 'Cream City's' longstanding relationship to America's larger criminal enterprise.

Within the pages of this book…

Get to know a man Fortune Magazine once named #17 on a list of fifty biggest Mafia bosses. It's the tale of a longstanding fixture in the annals of Milwaukee organized crime, a felonious mastermind who shared responsibility in instituting, exploiting and giving lucrative life to a now-commonplace term found in the proverbial lexicon of mob rackets – the *'skim.'* Meet Frank Balistrieri, a wiseguy better known within his own circles as 'Frankie Bals' and as you'll discover while traversing the pages herein - the bearer of a far more sinister moniker- the 'Mad Bomber.' Balistrieri's reign lasted for over three decades, and from the get-go he ruled the gambling underworld with an iron fist. Notwithstanding the powerful and infamous Chicago 'Outfit's' oversight (Chi Town being Milwaukee's benefactor), Frankie called the shots in his realm, as you'll find immortalized in some of his own quoted dialogue.   A 1964 surveillance audio tape captured 'Mr. Big' Balistrieri savoring the 'new' law of the lawless Milwaukee land. *"The bookies were not used to paying,"* recounted the recorded voice. *"Now they have to pay."* An undeniable example of his unwavering business acumen (besides the extreme 'car bombing' tactic of course), if ever there was one.

__Preface__

Wayne Clingman, 2019.

As a child growing up in Wisconsin, I heard stories about the Mafia but mostly from my great uncle who not only told stories about the Mob in Milwaukee but he also told me, his young grand-nephew, stories about Al Capone and his (my grand-uncle) fighting In Mexico in WWI (where he was gassed as a young kid). I thought of them as just more of the crazy stories that Uncle Roy told. He would die in his 90s in 1972. I loved him and his stories are a part of why I like history so much; our oral histories are all too soon forgotten, allowing the powers that be to change history into what they think is best

Jumping forward, we get to my wanting to do a film with Jason Love on the craziness in Milwaukee, thinking maybe something on the Outlaw biker wars, maybe something on Dahmer? However, after reading *The Milwaukee Mafia* by Gavin Schmitt, I knew I wanted to do the film on Frank Balistrieri (if only to find out more about what was going on with the mob in Milwaukee or how big it could really be).

Well, in doing the film (which you can find on Amazon), Frank turned out to be bigger than I had thought.

Far bigger.

Being me, I went for what I thought would be just a few pages from a Freedom of Information Act request. Then, 6 weeks later, here comes 1100 + pages about Frank, filled with tons of information and redacted pages/information.....

Gee, there is enough here to make a book...

__Introduction__

Frank Balistrieri died in Milwaukee on a chilly February day in 1993. It was a death by natural causes; two months earlier he was in St. Mary's Hospital for colon surgery. He was 74 at the time. In many ways it is a surprise that Balistrieri lived as long as he did, perhaps if it wasn't for his connections he would never have seen the '70s. Violence is a recurring theme in the story of Balistrieri's life, in many ways violence punctures the narrative – often it is what assures silence in Balistrieri's world.

And just what world was that?

Balistrieri was a puppet master, just outside of the frame yet controlling events that rippled out and affected not only the people of Milwaukee and the surrounding area but ultimately the American people as a whole. For many years Balistrieri was *the* man in control of organized crime in Milwaukee; in the August 6th, 1978 edition of the New York Times, the FBI released Frank Balistrieri's name along with the names of 29 other individuals suspected of being "crime leaders." That's Mafia with a capital M: the American-Italian Mafia, La Cosa Nostra.

If you're not from Milwaukee, you're probably wondering why you should care about the mob boss there. In popular culture, being from Milwaukee is often treated as a joke. For those in the city, the fascination makes more sense. Balistrieri has been a figure within Milwaukee for five decades, during which he rose to the top and earned the nickname "Mr. Big" (as well as "Mad Bomber," but we'll get to that in a moment). Throughout the years Balistrieri oversaw the night life in the city, controlling four of the bars and holding a monopoly in jukeboxes; maintained illegal gambling operations; and among other things was the guy robberies had to be okay'd through.

But again, that's local level, what about the rest of the world?

For them, most have already encountered Balistrieri's presence within film and haven't even realized it. Almost three years after Balistrieri died, Martin Scorsese's *Casino* (1995) was released into theatres. The film follows Robert De Niro as Sam "Ace" Rothstein. Ace is brought into Vegas by the Chicago Outfit to oversee the operations of several casinos which were based on the Stardust; the Fremont; and the Hacienda. The casinos are mob owned, money disappearing out the back. When things go wrong, Ace is almost killed by car bombing. Ace was only able to survive by a miracle of chance: a manufacturing defect in his model of car. Ace is based on the life of Frank Rosenthal, who really did survive a car bombing due to a defect in the model. It is suspected that Balistrieri called for that hit. He was called the "Mad Bomber," after all. And the money that poured out of those casinos went East, into the pockets of crime lords to fuel their excess and future schemes – or, that was the goal; the casino skim was to come crashing down on top of them.

The rise and fall of Balistrieri is a story of intriguing questions that highlights the power of violence, networking, and unrestrained greed. In structuring the book you have in your hands, I have decided to follow a mostly linear path. We begin where Balistrieri did and look into what we know about him before he caught the FBI's interest. This will bring us into Balistrieri's real education, the one he got from his father-in-law John Alioto, head of the Milwaukee crime family from '52–'61. We'll find that Frank was already a busy man, by the time he became the boss, when we take a look at the businesses he was running at this time. Balisteri took over the family at the end of '61 and we'll examine the tensions that seems to have caused. Then everything goes black and we'll explore why the FBI (our main source of information in this particular telling of Balistrieri's story) let Frank slip from their radars until '74 and his trip to Vegas. From there we'll take a look at the Vegas skim, how the law in Milwaukee was closing in, and his violent outlashes before he went to jail.

As mentioned, the primary source of information in this elling are several hundred FBI documents that chart how the Bureau continually failed to build a solid case against Balistrieri until the skim finally brought it all down. All lates, names and actions described within come from these documents unless otherwise stated. Where supporting

research has been used, it will be mentioned within the text.

It will also be noted when information is being obtained

from an informant, as that calls into question the validity of

the information unless otherwise noted to have been double

checked.

<u>One</u>

Frank Peter Balistrieri was born in Milwaukee on May 27th, 1918, just before noon. He was the first born child of Joseph Balistrieri, 23, and Benedetta Picciuerro, 20. Both of his parents had been born in Italy, making the baby Frank a first generation Italian-American. On paper Joseph worked as a garbage collector, Benedetta a housewife. Together the family lived in Milwaukee at 423 Van Buren Street. Frank would be followed by a brother, Peter, and a couple of sisters.

The Balistrieri family was a large one. If not the six at home then the extended family which included important figures like his uncle "Big Jim" Balistrieri from Kansas City, high ranking figure in the criminal milieu there. Frank

Peter Balistrieri was named after his grandfather, Frank Balistrieri. The elder Frank, who had also immigrated from Italy, got into the hauling business when he came to Milwaukee and even managed to score the contract for garbage hauling in the city. Grandpa Frank was father to seven sons who each honored his name by giving it to their first born sons. So in Frank Peter Balistrieri's family there were six other Frank Balistrieris to differentiate between. It is in this way that Frank Peter Balistrieri was not the only Frank Balistieri to rise to a place of power within the Italian-American criminal underworld, an uncle Frank Balistieri in San Diego was suspected of being one of the leaders of the syndicate within that city (along with uncle Peter).

Balistieri grew up surrounded by gangsters. While Joseph Balistieri doesn't appear often within the FBI's investigation in his son, there is plenty to suggest that he was complicit within the underworld business. The Mafia's conquest and exploitation of the sanitation industry has become a well known piece of the Cosa Nostra lore and Joseph Balistieri followed his father into the business; another important figure in Frank Balistieri's story, John Alioto, too, was a Milwaukee Department of Streets and Sanitation employee … on paper. Later, Joseph would be alleged to be fronting his son Frank in some of his business exploits, the FBI all but directly stating his implication.

It's clear that Frank took to lesson the importance of family, both from an Italian cultural standpoint and through the lens of organized crime. Throughout the years, family was to never be far away. Indeed, he would partner with his father in running the Badger State Boxing Club and his brother Peter would be a partner in the City Wide

Amusement Company (which controlled jukeboxes) and would be the name on the legal papers to let Frank run four taverns despite a city of Milwaukee ordinance that no one can own more than two taverns within the city. Family was important, not just because it collaborated in earning money. Family was power, and again and again it will prove to be family that enabled Frank to rise to power to become the head of the Milwaukee syndicate.

But like any growing boy in America, Frank needed a formal education. Something recognized officially, in parallel with his criminal training. That education was found first in Lincoln High School, from which he entered Marquette University, College of Liberal Arts, in September of 1935. His studies ended in June 1938, with ninety-eight semester hours and 135 qualitative points. Frank followed this by attending Marquette Law School, from which it was well known he had been a student but had never practiced law. Records at Marquette revealed to the FBI in 1958 that Frank Balistrieri was admitted as a regular student to the law school on July 5th, 1938, but that he was withdrawn due to sickness on January 18th, 1939. He returned on September 23rd, 1940, but was out again on March 26th, 1941. The records further revealed that Balistrieri only received grades for the first semester's enrollment. Thus, Balistrieri not only never practiced law but the question of whether he even studied it must be raised.

What was Balistrieri doing during that time and why was he kept on the records?

The answer to these questions remains unclear. However, Balistrieri was a busy man and the close of the 1930s would set him on the path to rise from a young criminal to the head of the local syndicate. That path was set before him, once again, through family. In particular, Frank Balistrieri's

marriage to Antonina Alioto on November 18, 1939, by the

Reverend Joseph A. Omesby, joined two powerful families

together: the Balistrieri's and the Alioto's. More importantly

than that, the marriage turned Frank into John Alioto's

son-in-law.

John Alioto was soon to be the most influential figure in

Frank Balistieri's life.

FBI documents reflect little interest given to Frank

Balistieri before Special Agent James E. McArdle put

together a report on him, dated January 7th, 1958, in which

the prime area of focus was on anti-racketeering. The report

would set off an avalanche of paperwork to follow, the case

moving from anti-racketeering to conspiracy to commit

murder, rip off the Welfare and Pension Plans Disclosure

Act (or WPPDA), and corruption of public officials. What

was began by McArdle would end up spreading over thousands of documents and a span of 25 years before Balistrieri served any real time. Beyond its importance as the foundation of the Frank Balistrieri case, what is most noteworthy in the report by McArdle is the lack of information on Balistrieri's criminal operations before the 1950s. This is first notable because, as an informant advised special agents on January 15, 1958, the Italian-American criminal organization of which Balistrieri was a part of would not accept members with a criminal record as such an individual would draw attention. With an "education" in law and no criminal record, Balistrieri clearly avoided attention for many years.

More intriguing is the second possibly it presents. As we'll explore more in depth in the next chapter, the same informants that readily pointed to Frank Balistreri as one of the most powerful figures in the Milwaukee Mafia were just as quick to suggest that his uncle "Big Jim" Balistrieri in Kansas City was where Frank found his strength and backing. While the Kansas City Balistrieri obviously was an important figure in giving Frank clout, this overlooks the importance of his father-in-law, John Alioto.

Alioto would take over as head of the Milwaukee Mafia after the Chicago Outfit had Sam Ferrara step down. Alioto would rule from '52–'61. The idea that Alioto's role was to prepare Frank for power has been suggested from many sources. That we see Frank begin business with taverns around the same time his father-in-law takes over is unsurprising, Alioto having a thumb in that pie already. Whether he took power to groom his son-in-law, or whether his son-in-law proved to be his most capable soldier is a question we may never know. What we do know is that the

1950s saw Balistrieri's true education.

And he was a grade A student.

<u>Two</u>

The FBI did not file a report on Frank Balistrieri until January 7th, 1958. However, as the report by Special Agent James E. McArdle lays out, his name had begun to show up in their investigations over the course of the decade. The first mention of Balistrieri was in October of 1950; an informant spoke to special agents regarding the then head of the Milwaukee Mafia, Sam Ferrara. The informant told agents that he considered Sam Ferrara and John Di Trapani, who would later get into beef with members of the Chicago Outfit and end up found dead slumped behind the wheel of his Cadillac, as members of the mafia. He also told them that Frank Balistrieri and his brother Peter were often in their company.

Frank disappears for over a year before showing back up November 14th, 1952, when an informant advised special agents that there appeared to be two financial factions in Milwaukee's Italian hoodlum element; one, according to them, is headed up by Phil Valley, Frank Balistrieri and Vincent Maniaci (names that will come up again shortly, and often).

On July 24, 1953, an informant claims Balistrieri is associated with a gambling establishment in the 1600 block on North Van Buren Street. As we'll see, Balistrieri has always been into gambling, sometimes to his own detriment rather than profit.

May 14, 1954, agents were advised that Balistrieri is a member of the "syndicate" in Milwaukee along with the Aliotos, Aliotas, Di Amatos, Mike Albano, Frank La Galbo, and Phil Valley.

December of the same year the FBI is advised that Balistrieri would soon take over management of the Tic-Toc night club in Milwaukee.

As the decade progressed, it became clearer and clearer that Frank Balistrieri was somebody important within the criminal underground of Milwaukee but the FBI still didn't open a file on him until 1958. And this is despite the fact that in October of 1955, members of the Milwaukee Police Department advised Special Agents Richard C. Thompson and Frank J. Larkin, the same two special agents to have gathered the information on Balistrieri thus far, that they considered Balistrieri and Phil Valley to be the two most powerful members of the Mafia operating in Milwaukee.

At this same time the FBI was told that the Milwaukee Police Department had heard rumors that Balistrieri was responsible for the bombing of Fazio's Restaurant and

Tavern earlier in the year. The restaurant on North Jackson Street had previously been the Tic-Toc night club that Balistrieri had shown interest in acquiring. Though this wasn't new information to the FBI, as informants had already told them on July 13th and August 24th that Balistrieri was believed responsible because he was pissed off at the Fazio family for buying the property. People close to Balistrieri, that one would have assumed to have been his friends, will again and again show anger and frustration at his actions; actions such as ordering bombings and killings without any regard for how they will ripple out and affect those around him. They consider him to be dangerous, temperamental, and uncontrollable.

But isn't that kinda what we want in a Mafia boss? That is, we the viewing public that reads books like the one you are engaged with currently or watch films like *Goodfellas*

(1990) or *Casino*. In reading about Balistrieri's life, one can't help but be reminded of Al Capone – if for no reason other than to consider the way his violence had already been, if not glorified, mythologized by film treatments such as *Scarface* (1932), along with uncountable more. Balistrieri wasn't just recreating the violence depicted in the movies, however; he was associating and doing business with the generation that grew up under Capone. Balistrieri wasn't just playing at being a gangster like the movies; Balistrieri was injecting himself into the world of mythology itself and that could only be done *through* violence.

During that August 24th session, that same informant advised that Balistrieri is very friendly with Marshall Caifano, who was near the top of the Chicago criminal element on the near West side.

Again, the connections that Balistrieri formed through friends and family continue to help him.

There's "Big Jim" Balistrieri, his uncle, out in Kansas City.

There's father-in-law John Alioto, who at this time was the big boss.

Friends out in Chicago.

More family out on the West coast.

At home there are tight binds between his associates like Phil Valley, a local agent of Milwaukee's Cooks, Waiters and Bartenders Union.

And one of the more frequent characters in the story of Balistrieri's life, his cousin Bustiano Vito Balestrere, aka Buster.

Buster plays the role of Balistrieri's bodyguard and legman. Buster was reputed to have been kicked out of the

Kansas City organization. Though it is never made explicitly clear, the FBI documents link Buster's expulsion to assault and battery charges against him from 1941. Though these were later dropped, the FBI seems to suggest that Buster's criminal record got him kicked out of Kansas but the truth remains unclear. Among the other possibilities, such as Buster getting on the wrong side of the Kansas crew, is the possibility that Buster was a gift. A body guard and loyal soldier from Frank's uncle Big Jim Balistrieri of Kansas. This is given some weight considering a later trip to Kansas City we'll see Buster undertaking.

The community that Balistrieri found himself a part of is one in which he has been given a privileged position through his biological connections that he then leveraged to gain contacts and networks all throughout Milwaukee and the surrounding areas. In doing so, Balistrieri was able to get in tight with local politicians, business owners, police department members and more (as we shall see). This web of connection is one in which figures will come and go but together all work to form a kind of social protection behind which Balistrieri is able to maneuver from to gain, and guarantee, his position of power.

On May 13, 1957, Milwaukee Police Department advises special agents that an informant linked Balistrieri with possibly fencing stolen furs from a robbery on November 20, 1956. During this period in time, the FBI director will point to this being the only thing even close to a lead that the Milwaukee branch has on Balistrieri, with an almost insultatory tone – the director seems to suggest that Milwaukee is barking up the wrong tree and wasting their time. The underworld might know that Balistrieri was the one to approve or disapprove robberies but the FBI had no way of proving this fact.

That's the thing with Balistrieri and, in a larger degree, the mafia. The higher the rank a member is, the more insolation there is to protect against the smaller level crimes. Balistrieri was not involved in the bombing of the Fazio restaurant ... directly, in a physical capacity. In the same way, Balistrieri is not the one performing the robberies. Balistrieri, at this particular moment in time, is like that of a medieval knight. He has his dominion, those that work under him, but he is still beholden to his liege. In this case, Balistrieri's liege is John Alioto, to which Balistrieri owes a part of his income. Below Balistrieri are those, like Buster, that do the legwork and put themselves at the highest risk through direct involvement. But their liege is Balistrieri, and so they insulate him from risk. The higher you rise, the more layers there are to peel back to prove culpability.

On June 3, an anonymous tip let agents know that Balistrieri was bringing in four girls from Minneapolis to work in his establishments, the Melody Room and the Downtowner, both of which were known for putting on strip shows (with progressively more lax rules on exhibitionism as time progresses). Though the tip giver could not say if they were being brought in as entertainers or as prostitutes, they certainly implied the former.

Finally, the last piece of catch up prior to that first report, was an informant who, on January 2, 1958, advised that Balistrieri is closely tied with Phil Valley, local agent of Milwaukee's Cooks, Waiters and Bartenders Union (giving the Milwaukee syndicate an insider in regards to union business) and said to be one of the two most powerful figures in Milwaukee (along with Balistrieri). The informant continued to explain that Balistrieri had on occasion implied to restaurant and tavern owners that they could avoid union troubles by playing ball with him. Thus, Balistrieri made claim to speak on behalf of not just Phil Valley, as agent, but on behalf of the Cooks, Waiters and Bartenders Union as a whole. A chilling suggestion of just how corrupt the union truly was.

And with that final piece, we have caught up to what the FBI had known about Balistrieri as they prepared their January 7th report.

And it wasn't really much.

Just what have we seen?

Balistrieri has been accused of strong arm tactics, implying that working with him will save hardships or straight up blowing up the competition. He was suggested to have his thumb in gambling, extortion, prostitution. We know that by this point he was legally running two taverns and was the man behind the curtain of at least two others. But all of this was suggestions, where was the evidence? Severely lacking; it was rumors, suggestions, he-said, she-said. But solid proof? Proof that you can point at and say, "Frank Peter Balistrieri did this crime and here is how," proof like that …. Well, it just didn't exist.

They didn't have a damned thing.

Throughout this period, Balistrieri was still involved in the jukebox and gaming machine business. Some heat was coming down on him regarding his handling of the business. This is evidenced by the fact that Balistrieri saw the need to approach a special detail, that had been set up to look into accusations that he strong armed his machines into establishments, so he could speak to them himself in a declaration of his innocence. Balistrieri said his peace and nothing appears to have become of it.

Though throughout the fifties and pushing onward, it's clear that Balistrieri begins to step away from this particular source of revenue. Perhaps his encounter with the special detail made him rethink the endeavour: Was it worth the level of heat for the profit they generated? Maybe it was better to own some taverns rather than trying to exploit a handful of tavern owners.

Following that train of thought, records reflect that Balistrieri was the president of Ben-Kay, Inc, a company which was formulated and chartered on December 22, 1952, to operate the Downtowner Tavern. Frank was also president of Hotel Roosevelt, Inc, in which he kept offices and operated the Melody Room, a nightclub, and the Grant Bar, a tavern.

Milwaukee Trade Winds, Inc, operated the Trade Winds Tavern and Restaurant and Peter Balistrieri, Frank's brother, was president. Frank was vice president. Peter was also the president of Towner Tavern, Inc, which ran the Towner Tavern and Restaurant.

Frank Balistrieri was legally the president for the companies, Ben-Kay, Inc, and Hotel Roosevelt, Inc, which oversaw the Melody Room, the Grant Bar and the Downtowner. However, witnesses and employees again and again state that Frank would sign papers, give orders and paychecks, and generally was known as the man in charge at all of the above mentioned establishments. Regardless of whether it was his brother Peter's club or not, Balistrieri was still recognized by all those involved in the running of the clubs as the owner. Based on the interviews present in the FBI's materials, it would seem that people assumed the ownership to be one of the Balistrieri family's rather than either Frank's or Peter's alone.

It's hard not to take notice of the fact that Balistrieri got into the tavern and nightclub game the same year his father-in-law, John Alioto, became the head of the Milwaukee syndicate. Alioto was perhaps handing off some of his responsibility, being too busy now in running the Milwaukee family to be able to keep up with the demands of the nightclub business. But if this is the case, Alioto didn't need to look any further than his son-in-law, a figure whose trust was guaranteed as if they shared the same blood, to find someone to pick up his slack.

The fact that Frank was involved in four taverns (though five technically, two were legally covered under one incorporated business) caused problems. Milwaukee Police Department began efforts, around July of 1957, to block

Frank from being able to acquire any more businesses within the field and it became an issue, not just between Frank and the Police Department but between Frank and syndicate. This little piece of information, a mostly legal battle in which Balistrieri attempted to slip through loopholes in the law and in which the Police Department struggled to plug them before they were found, seems a rather uninteresting note in his life but becomes one of the keys in pointing towards the discontent that Balistrieri apparently brought in his wake.

Balistrieri was damned good at getting around laws, too. One of the ways that Balistrieri got around them is highlighted perfectly in how Balistrieri controlled both the Melody Room and the Downtowner. The Melody Room was part of the Hotel Roosevelt at 412 W. Wells St. Just down the road, at 340 W. Wells St. was the Downtowner. Laws prohibited the female dancers of these clubs from conversing with the audience, a way of preventing the performers at the club from swindling men into buying more drinks. Less drinks meant less money in Balistrieri's pocket.

Balistrieri got around this law by sending the girls from the Melody Room to the Downtowner and the girls from the Downtowner to the Melody Room to act as "B" girls. In this way, the girls legally were not involved as employees of the business within which they were soliciting drinks but the money all went back into the same pocket.

Balistrieri's pocket.

The Melody Room and the Downtowner are, at various times and from the mouths of various people, described as strip joints. With informants making suggestions like how Balistrieri, Phil Valley and those guys were suckers for a female and that, despite being married, Balistrieri was in no way faithful to his wife, it might not be such a far stretch to wonder if Frank was into prostitution as well.

Clearly the idea had already been floated by informants, as was suggested when Balistrieri brought women in from Minneapolis. While there is nothing within the FBI files to disprove this accusation, a careful reading suggests that Balistrieri did not use the women at his clubs for general prostitution but that they were expected to service himself and important friends/colleagues when they were in town and so were still treated in a misogynist and belittling way that is all to familiar to modern readers in the wake of the #MeToo movement.

The files also suggest that during this period Balistrieri had been or begun seeing a mistress, a young woman that one of her neighbours referred to as "very hard and rough."

Balistrieri paid for her apartment and was often seen to be visiting the premises.

When it came to business, Balistrieri ran everything out of an office at the top of the Hotel Roosevelt. He had even had the place remodeled in '56. But the city had been looking to purchase the property from the owner of the premises and were in talks to demolish the building.

Despite doing everything he could to stall them, Balistrieri also moved the books and ledgers relating to his various businesses from the Hotel Roosevelt into the apartment he rented for his mistress. The FBI would target her apartment as a site of interest in regards to getting some form of surveillance on the inside but, since she was almost always there and Balistrieri came and left at any and all hours of the night, it was decided after a time that it was too risky an operation for them to undertake.

A week after that first FBI report, an informant did his best to lay out the score regarding how the Milwaukee Mafia was structured and ran. John Alioto was the head of the Milwaukee crew, with Milwaukee itself being under the supervision of the Italian organization in Chicago that was headed up by Tony Acardo. Acardo gave Alioto his orders, according to the informant.

Balistrieri was Alioto's lieutenant and would handle fixes with the Milwaukee Police Department and the local District Attorney's office. Balistrieri would also finger crimes, being the guy you had to talk to and get approval from before committing any large burglary. Other informants would continue to make suggestions that Balistrieri was politically connected and that it offered him a level of protection.

Also in the Milwaukee crew was confirmed August "Augie" Maniaci, Vito Aiello and his brother John Aiello, who had many contacts among the various fences the Mafia used to sell their stolen goods. The FBI files on Balistrieri make little reference to these three's roles within the syndicate, except to suggest that Augie was within the top five most powerful members of the Milwaukee hoodlum element. However, they do appear as forces that stand in opposition to Balistrieri's rise to power – however, as far as opposition goes, they don't manage to prevent Balistrieri in the least.

Buster and Bito Balistere, cousins of Frank, were originally members of the Kansas City organization but had been kicked out and were now part of Balistrieri's crew.

There's also mention at this point of several redacted names paying protection money to Balistrieri, as well as the crew having an in with John Polcyn while he had been the Chief of Police in Milwaukee from 1945 until 1957.

Of note was the fact that Balistrieri won't okay a crime if the risk for heat is too high, or if it goes against business and friendship values – he would not okay crimes against friends or partners, there were some lines a man just doesn't cross and were clearly drawn in the sand with a sense of morality in mind.

Avoiding heat, however, was just good business.

The FBI continued to gather information and put together a profile on Balistieri. To that end, on January 31, 1958, an informant advised FBI agents that Balistrieri is second only to John Alioto and will eventually succeed him, with Augie Maniaci the next after Balistrieri. But less than a month later, February 27, agents were advised that the Milwaukee organization was in the process of dropping Balistrieri due to the bad publicity that had been kicked up the previous year in regards to his operating more than two taverns with

Milwaukee and the Milwaukee Police Department's efforts to block his acquisition of more.

That within a month Balistrieri would have went from second in charge to about to be dropped is a little hard to believe. Was there such a serious shift within the organization in less than a month? It's possible, of course, but highly doubtful – the time frame is too short, considering the bad publicity originated in the previous year. What's more likely is that different informants reflect different rumors and that Balistrieri, being a decisive figure that provoked a range of feelings in the people around him, was spoken about differently depending on who one was listening to.

It's also reflective of the way the FBI had to gather information, reaching out to informants where they could and trying to put together a story out of a mass of "he-said, she-said" that was often third or fourth hand, let alone second. This problem with informants is made worse when one considers the possibility that any informant is at risk of being a plant, a deliberate attempt at misinformation to leave the FBI treading water. Whether or not Balistrieri had plants is a good question, considering how politically connected he was. It's more than likely that Balistrieri would eventually catch wind that the FBI was investigating him, though the likelihood of a plant this early is low.

At least, it's low for a plant that Balistrieri deliberately placed. But the investigation into Balistrieri spun off from investigations into other members of the hoodlum element in Milwaukee, any of which might have been able to plant an informant previously to support them and their cause; this could be done by pointing blame away from the figure in question and pointing the FBI towards others' crimes and activities that are damaging the figure in question's earnings. This remains a possibility and leaves open a further question: Did any of the informants have a bone to pick with Balistrieri?

Accordingly, Frank Balistrieri was either the second most important person in the Milwaukee syndicate or a nobody that was about to be dropped. The agents in Milwaukee suspected it was the first and requested mail coverage on his home and places of employment that March of '58. The home office clearly thought it was the latter option, however, and they denied the requests. As far as the home office was concerned, the agents in Milwaukee had only been able to make a suggestion that Balistrieri might have helped fence some stolen furs or used suggestive language to help his business dealings.

There was not enough to go on with Balistrieri, the home office said.

The agents in Milwaukee set out to prove the home office wrong and, by May 2, Milwaukee selected Frank Peter Balistrieri as the individual with the best potential for penetrating into the Italian-American criminal element in the city. At this point, the FBI was beginning a major effort to crack down on hoodlums across America called the Top Hoodlum Program.

On November 14, 1957, in the small town of Apalachin, New York State Troopers noticed a large number of expensive cars with out of state licence plates. It would turn out that they belonged to Mafia leaders from across the country. The media fallout of this event would force the FBI to admit, finally in a firm manner, that the Mafia was operating in America on a national scale. Dealing with the media fallout of the event, J. Edgar Hoover created the Top Hoodlum Program which would consist of surveillance and coverage of syndicate leaders.

FBI surveillance was set on Balistrieri, in accordance with the Top Hoodlum Program's guidelines, and found his days to be remarkably similar. Balistrieri would leave his house between 10:30am and noon, proceeding directly to the Trade Winds Tavern where he would remain until early evening. Later in the evenings, Balistrieri would head to the Hotel Roosevelt to oversee operations at the Melody Room and the Downtowner (where the interchange of female entertainers between the bars was witnessed by agents). Afterwards he would head home to sleep. Except for that interchange of entertainers, the FBI witnessed nothing linking Balistrieri with the crimes that informants had pointed them towards.

All talk, no results. Balistrieri was careful for someone considered hot headed and impulsive. His careful nature is exemplified by his behaviour while at the Hotel Roosevelt office.

When it came to Mr. Balistrieri's stay at the Hotel Roosevelt, one of the front desk workers said, he had a protocol in case he ever had guests or visitors of any kind. The front desk would telephone Mr. Balistrieri in his third floor office. Shortly thereafter, Mr. Balistrieri would come downstairs to meet the caller. Depending on what kind of business was on hand, Balistrieri would either speak with them there in the lobby of the hotel or in the Melody Room since it was situated within the Roosevelt. This would happen without fail unless it was a very personal friend or a very important and personal matter.

Balistrieri was very, very selective about who he let up into his office.

Those informants the FBI had gathered had also been mentioning, early that May, that they had been hearing through the grapevine about some unrest in the Milwaukee syndicate.

It would seem that Frank Balistrieri was proving unpopular, with Augie Maniaci, Vito Aiello and Walter "Blackie" Brocca wanting to replace him in the organization. None of the men were willing to touch Balistrieri as long as John Alioto was alive for fear of Alioto's retaliation though.

That Augie and Brocca turned against Frank is interesting. That Augie was third in line to power behind Balistrieri suggests the desire not just to eliminate someone known for catching heat for but a desire to make a power play, as it was thought Alioto would soon be headed out West. Brocca's motives, on the other hand, are unknown.

During the same conversation that revealed these rumors, it was mentioned that Brocca was thought to have been the wheelman used by Buster and Di Salvo in the bombing of Fazio's. That Brocca would help with "the Mad Bomber's" dynamiting of the restaurant three years earlier and then be debating killing him now is surprising, though reflective of the ebb and flow of trust/violence within the underworld.

And it would have to be murder, as there was no other way to get rid of such a violent character like Balistrieri. If they feared retaliation from Alioto, they must have been debating killing Balistrieri, otherwise it would be Balistrieri himself that they would have to fear – and God save them if their attempt were to fail...

By 1959, the investigation into Balistrieri was getting nowhere. Sure, information was still coming in like the informant who, on June 12, advised that it's difficult to tell who was the leader in Milwaukee at the moment, either John Alioto, Frank Balistrieri or Frank La Galbo.

John Alioto, the informant added, was for a number of years recognized as being the leader and was always shown the respect that comes with that position but, they suggested, Alioto was probably not the leader anymore and so it was a toss up between the two Franks. Perhaps a dual leadership.

July 4 they were being told that while one of the two Franks was still suspected of being in charge, Phil Valley was also carrying a lot of influence. However, Valley was still afraid of Balistrieri and thus would consult him before acting.

Balistrieri's hand in gambling was also still being suggested by informants at this point, as well as Balistrieri's desire to enter into a private brand whiskey bottling business that he was setting aside a budget for $250,000 to get into with a contact in the Teamsters Union.

But other than some accusations that lacked evidential weight, there was nothing proving Balistrieri's underhanded dealings.

And so, on August 21, 1959, the FBI closed the case on Frank Balistrieri, citing the investigations failure to develop a violation of federal or local law which was not already known to local law enforcement.

Three

It wouldn't stay closed for very long, however; less than a year later, June 1, 1960, the file would be opened back up. The primary reason for the new file was to explore why Buster Balistere and Steve Di Salvo made a trip to Kansas City (as representatives of Frank). This report, though quite short, lays out what had been heard through informants and the grapevine in regards to Balistrieri since August 21, 1959. Within the file are four of the key areas that we will be exploring within this chapter.

First, there is the question of the Kansas City trip. Why did Buster and Di Salvo head to Kansas City? The FBI never answers this conclusively but things around Balistrieri were beginning to become heated. With power starting to become an issue in the Milwaukee area (and with their relationship to Chicago, which we'll touch on shortly), it's important to remember that Balistrieri had close to ties to the Kansas mob through his uncle – a powerbase from which Balistrieri could gain backing in a time of need. The FBI would not identify the reason for the trip, but they do clearly set out the pressures that Balistrieri had come to be facing at this time.

The second area of focus is on Balistrieri's legal businesses. As we will see, it is those legal businesses that will become the biggest thorn in Balistrieri's side at this point in time. From owed back taxes to legal battles and a short prison stint, are all on Frank's horizon here.

The third area will be on Balistrieri's gambling operations. By all accounts, Frank was getting more involved in the illegal gambling scene. While this gives us a better understanding of what Balistrieri was up to at this point in time, it pays off more in the long run as gambling operations would prove yet another thorn in Balistrieri's side – only this thorn wouldn't start bleeding for almost two decades. But the gambling operations also point towards the violence that Balistrieri conjurered forth through his orders.

The final area carries this theme of violence forward by looking at the murder of Izzy Pogrob on January 6, 1960. We will see the finger of blame in Izzy's slaying come to rest on Balistrieri. Further, Pogrob's nightclub, The Brass Rail, would be suggested as one of the clubs that Balistrieri controlled (this time with Rudolph Porchetta on the papers as legal owner of both The Brass Rail and the nearby La Scala restaurant).

Looking to those legal businesses, one would suspect them to be a cushion for Balistrieri in regards to his illegal activities. They offer both a way to bring in more money than he should be (as seen by his use of B-girls and his ghostly ownership of additional venues beyond the two he was legally the face of) and a way to bring that extra money into his bookkeeping to hide his illegal earnings. However, Balistrieri's experience here demonstrates an important lesson in regards to criminal activities: keep your taxes up to date.

You'd think the story of Al Capone would've been clear in Balistrieri's mind. Capone, that most legendary of gangsters, was brought down in the end because of tax evasion. The warning was clear as day and by all means one would expect it to have taken on mythological significance: if the best can fall, so shall we all. But perhaps it was a disregard of history, or just the stubborn confidence (or big-dickishness) of the career criminal, that saw Balistrieri ignoring the lessons of history – and thus was he doomed to repeat them.

The Milwaukee Journal, April 14, 1960, carried an article entitled "Balistrieri Firm Hit by Tax Lien," which provided the following information. A tax lien was filed against the Ben-Kay, Inc, which was running the Downtowner. The tax lien was to the amount of $6,598.30 and covered excise taxes from the first quarter of 1957 through to the third quarter of 1959. To put this into perspective, using an inflation calculator puts Balistrieri's owed taxes at $56,384.72 in 2019 dollars, which is a lot of money to be owing over the two in a half years the lien covered. But that wasn't the end of it.

Another lien was placed against the Hotel Roosevelt, Inc to the tune of $454.03, or $3,879.84 in 2019. This must have been particularly bothersome considering that the Hotel

Roosevelt had been purchased from the land owners by the City of Milwaukee in January of 1960; Balistieri was forced to vacate the premises by March 1, and the building was subsequently torn down.

What must have been even more bothersome, indeed damned troubling, was that they were still coming after the taxes for a building that no longer existed. Worse yet, it was in the Hotel Roosevelt that Balistrieri had ran the Melody Room which was also hit with a tax lien. This one for $4,715.46 (or $40,295.21).

In total, Balistrieri owed $11,767.79, which adjusts for inflation to the impressive $100,559.77. It's no surprise that on April 18th an informant told FBI agents that Balistrieri was indicating to his friends and associates that he would soon be going to jail because of these taxes.

Funny enough, despite the issues with taxes that Balistrieri was facing, informants in late June of 1960 were advising agents that Balistrieri was looking to get deeper into the tavern game. With the loss of the Hotel Roosevelt and the Melody Room, informants said that the former Scenic Lounge (now Henri's) was actually a front for Balistrieri (with Buster acting as protection). Interesting, at this point Henri's was in the process of booking some high costing guests through talent agencies across America – however, Balistrieri barely promoted any of the events they were at, which only serves to raise questions as to the point of hiring them at all (with the clearest possibility being either a play for legitimacy or a way of laundering money). Henri's, FBI agents were informed, was expected to soon be run as a strip-tease joint with dancers interchaging as B-girls with the Downtowner.

The informant stated that it was only through Balistrieri's political ties that he was able to get licensing for Henri's, furthering the ties between Balistrieri and the political sector of Milwaukee. (Another tie would come in January of 1962 when spotted hanging on the wall in Balistrieri's home was an autographed photograph of the Attorney General with the inscription, "To Frankie from Bob.")

As it turns out, Balistrieri knew more than the Milwaukee Journal had in regards to his taxes though: he actually owned even more, because they hadn't grabbed the numbers hit against Peter Balistrieri's bars, which were bouncing back against Frank, regardless. Peter had asked the federal court to restrain the IRS and the Justice Department from questioning him about the tax liabilities of his taverns until they gave him back his books and records. However, Peter's motion to be able to use the books that the IRS presently possessed was turned down by Judge Robert E. Tehan on the ground that "the tax assessment and collection powers of the government are to be rarely, if at any time, interfered with by the injunctive arm of the court. It is fundamental that the country's collecting power would be brought to a halt if that power were restrained."

These taxes would be the first thing to put Balistrieri behind bars. It wouldn't be his only conviction over the course of the 74 years he lived. There is some confusion, at least in the FBI files, regarding Frank's prison sentence; this is most reflective of the way that the FBI had lost sight of Balistrieri as the sixties progressed. A newly opened file in 1973 states that Balistrieri was convicted in June, 1971, in regards to filing fraudulent tax returns, and was released a year and a day later. However, Jay C. Ambler of AmericanMafia.com puts Balistrieri's conviction in March,

1967. According to Ambler, Balistrieri served two years and was *released* in June, 1971. Ambler's suggestion of 1967 would seem to be corroborated by a court of appeals document – United States V. Frank Peter Balistrieri, 403 F.2d 472 (7th Cir. 1968) – dated December 31st, 1968, which denied Balistieri a rehearing.

That the 1960s were so wild and that Balistrieri spent the end of them in prison, are two reasons that point towards a large gap in time we will encounter in the FBI documents moving forward. That the FBI had its hands full with a great many high profile, well documented investigations may be to blame for the odd dates that show back up in regards to Balistrieri's stint in jail. Also to blame, perhaps, is that it was a new decade and new investigators – could it be that with the changing of the guard, as it were, that information about Balistirieri and investigations into his crimes had gotten muddled? Unfortunately, it's a question that we may never know the answer to.

But let's turn our attention back to those years that began the sixties so as to take a look at Balistrieri's involvement within gambling operations in and around the Milwaukee area.

In February of 1960, the FBI was advised by an informant that Buster Balistrere had renewed his acquaintanceship with known gambler Johnny Rizzo. Rizzo was known to the local police as a gambler and one informant would only refer to him as "that lecherous old man." Rizzo was suspected, with the informant seemingly corroborating, of running a gambling game in Kenosha.

According to the informant, this game was held on behalf of Frank Balistrieri.

What's more, the informant suggests that Balistrieri had been given part of the Antioch, Illinois, territory for gambling and was training some of his men before they start operating there. Unfortunately, the FBI does not appear to have followed up on this particular claim; though, this may be due to a Grand Jury investigation into gambling in Waukegan, Illinois, that was apparently driving gamblers out of Illinois and into the Kenosha area.

Furthering the link between Balistrieri and corruption in local law enforcement, the informant was unable to finger anyone in particular but claimed the game could not be run unless Balistrieri was paying off the police to protect it.

A later FBI report has a redacted individual stating that Balistrieri's mob moved into Kenosha by buying out the crap games and gambling operations previously held there by Louis Greco. Balistrieri's game refused to allow people of color to attend the Friday night games anymore. Steve Di Salvo is cited as frequently being spotted next to the Greco Restaurant in Kenosha on Friday nights, thus given some grounding to claims that he was often overseeing them.

Come March 16, the same informant was advising FBI agents that the heat was on in Kenosha in regards to gambling but that Johnny Rizzo continued to run the game there. The game was still running by August 23, as an informant stated the game continues to be run by Rizzo, with Buster and Di Salvo helping to supervise the game. Balistrieri, of course, being the true controller.

And Balistrieri ran things with an iron fist, as demonstrated by his way of retrieving gambling debts.

On the night of May 12, an unnamed patron of Skinny's Tavern, near Zion, Illinois, stepped outside and was immediately fired at by unknown assailants with a shotgun.

The informant belaying the story informed FBI agents that the unnamed patron was a former resident of Kenosha and that he owed the Kenosha gambling element a debt. The informant shows no doubt whatsoever in pinning the assault to Balistrieri's crew.

However, at some point between August of 1960 and April of 1961, the heat relating to the gambling must have been getting to Balistrieri and his crew. An informant on April 7 advised that Rizzo had reopened the dice game in Kenosha and feels that the heat is off. Though they are still operating on a limited basis. Accordingly, Buster and Di Salvo continue to supervise the game as Balistrieri's representatives with Frank definitely having a big piece in the game. Was the heat brought from local law enforcement or was it a result of hoodlums from Waukegan bringing the heat with them when they showed up?

Either way, the heat didn't stay away for very long because by July of 1961 informants were advising that Di Salvo and Buster no longer oversaw the games due to fear of law enforcement. However, it was noted that Buster's little brother was now taking over the role of overseer.

Whatever the reason, Balistrieri did not stay away from gambling for very long. Did the gambling just bring in too much money to take account of the risk? Or did Balistrieri just enjoy the racket? Whatever the answer, it's clear that Balistrieri and gambling go hand in hand – eventually, like his taxes, gambling will take Balistrieri a step too far in the eyes of the law.

But that's a story for another chapter.

Before we move into the Pogrob killing, let's take a brief moment to explore some of the other events that Balistrieri was involved with (or thought to be involved with) during this period of 1960-1961.

Balistrieri was still seeing his mistress at this time, according to FBI observation, and at the start of 1961 they located the new apartment that Balistrieri had moved her into. Balistrieri's photo was shown to the deskman who confirmed that he was the gentleman who would come visit the young lady at her apartment therein.

Balistrieri was often observed carrying books into the apartment. The FBI wanted them, badly. But like the previous apartment he had rented for his mistress, it seemed impregnable. This was confirmed when on the rare opportunity where she had left the apartment building to go out somewhere, the FBI found that the master key for the building no longer fit the apartment's locks.

There was still hope of getting their hands on Balistrieri's garbage, however. The building was designed with trash shoots and it was hoped by the FBI that they would be able to retrieve some paperwork after disposal. This was quickly proven unlikely as it was observed that Balistrieri or his mistress always threw a match down with their garbage. This match would light the incinerator, as it was designed to be able to do so from any floor of the building.

In the end, after a ton of surveillance, the FBI would never be able to get between Balistrieri, his mistress, and his ledgers.

During September of 1960, informants indicated that Balistrieri was looking to get into the business of aluminum roofs and siding and in this connection had begun a relationship with Valley Builders Supply. According to informants, Balistrieri was joined on this venture by "like minded" men and were muscling into the business locally.

Balistrieri looked to be getting involved in yet another business venture according to Chief of Police William Wolcott of the Brookfield Police Department when he spoke to FBI agents on August 15. According to him another tavern/club called The Volcano was being expensively remodelled and that, according to rumors his department had been hearing, Frank Balistrieri had an interest in the place. Balistrieri shared that financial interest with Frank Accardo, of Chicago, and one Ralph Capone of Mercer, Wisconsin.

It's worth noting just how many businesses Balistrieri had under his belt at this time. Jukeboxes; boxing matches; bars; nightclubs; a hotel; a company for producing (and another for marketing) a gun that shoots bubbles; interest in private whiskey labeling and now aluminum roofing. Balistrieri gives the illusion of a highly knowledgeable and successful businessman.

However, in April of 1961 when Balistrieri was to take a more active role in Para Corp (made to produce that bubble gun), an unnamed member of the organization reported to agents that Balistrieri had no idea what he was doing and that he, the informant, had no idea how Balistrieri could run a successful nightclub – let alone several.

If Balistrieri wasn't a businessman, then how was he able to keep so many businesses afloat? The answer is twofold. Fold the first: Hire people that know what they are doing. Balistrieri was a busy, busy man, clearly, and if you want to keep a business going you make sure you hire someone that knows what the hell they're doing. Fold the second: Balistrieri's illegal business made money, a lot of money, plain and simple.

Gambling, taxes, business … Balistrieri had a lot on the go during these two years and we haven't even gotten into the Pogrob killing yet. Pogrob was a local nightclub owner whose death was to cause a tidepool of ripples in the opinions and power structure surrounding Balistrieri; included among those is the claim that Balistrieri took over control of the Brass Rail club following Pogrob's death (by purchasing it from Pogrob's living brother).

On January 6, 1960, a Wednesday, Izzy Pogrob closed up the Brass Rail around 3am and decided to take his employees out for an early breakfast at the nearby Belmont Hotel. Izzy loved food almost as much as he loved money, and so he had himself a large meal while thumbing through a wad of bills estimated at around $1500. A waitress of the Belmont Hotel's Cafe reported to the Milwaukee Journal that a mysterious man with long dyed blond hair had sat near the group eavesdropping and had then conferred with two men at a nearby booth.

Izzy finished his meal and left in good spirits.

It would be the last time that Izzy Pogrob was seen alive.

Izzy's white Cadalliac was found the next day, the front splattered with blood.

Later that day, his body would be found.

Izzy Pogrob had been left in a drainage ditch in Mequon, off of highway 167. Izzy had been blindfolded and shot nine times in and around his head.

To this date, the murder has never been solved.

But the informants the FBI gathered tell a different story, one in which the murder isn't a mystery at all but a signed statement from none other than Frank Peter Balistieri.

The first time the FBI heard about the Pogrob killing in relation to Balistrieri was June 8, just over five months after the slaying occurred. According to the informant, a person named Frank Stelloh may shortly be released from state prison on parole. Apparently, he was picked up for questioning in regards to the Pogrob killing. Stelloh volunteered to take a lie detector test but Balistieri gave Stelloh orders specifically not to.

The informant believed that Balistrieri wanted Stelloh to remain in prison until the heat had worn off the Pogrob case. That heat was more than just the local law enforcement asking questions or picking Stelloh up, though. As it were to turn out, the Pogrob murder and Frank's ascent to head of the Milwaukee Mafia occured simultaneously with the one affecting the other – mirrors facing mirrors.

On June 8, informants advised agents that Balistrieri was still the right-hand man of John Alioto but that Alioto's son, Joe Alioto, had been making a great many of the decisions for his father and that the hoodlums in the area are now contacting Joe rather than John on most things. However, if a job is large enough they will still contact the elder Alioto.

So, at this point in time we are seeing Balistrieri still as the second hand man but the question of who controls power is being confused in the eyes of the law. Is it Balistrieri, the mad bomber that has been rising up the ranks? Was it John Alioto, Balistieri's father-in-law and the head of the organization since 1952? Or was it Joe Alioto, a name that had never come up in their reports until now? Either way, what is still clear is that Alioto is in change in some capacity and that Balistrieri is near the top.

On June 30, informants were bringing back news of a major shift in the underworld. Informants never told agents why but stated that there was talk that the Chicago syndicate was "down" on Balistrieri. One informant went on to say that this is serious because it had also been said that Phil

Valley, long time Balistrieri acquaintance and local agent for

the Milwaukee's Cooks, Waiters and Bartenders Union, has

washed his hands of Balistrieri and that the two of them

were said to now be battling.

Balistrieri was now facing enemies from inside

Milwaukee itself, as well as the disapprovement of Chicago,

their nominal "boss." However, great periods of silence

undercut the narrative when reading the FBI's reports and

the next important step in this particular thread of

Balistrieri's story wouldn't arrive until November 29.

Informants advised agents that John Alioto has stepped

down as leader of the Italian-American syndicate in

Milwaukee in favor of Frank Peter Balistrieri, thus making

Balistrieri the leader. This made one informant

incomfortable, they had said, because he does not like

seeing Balistrieri move into a policy making position of any kind because Balistrieri's judgement is not very good.

To make his point, the informant pointed to the Izzy Pogrob killing. There could be no doubt, according to the informant, that Balistrieri had ordered Buster, Steve Di Salvo and Frank Stelloh to put Izzy in his place. It would seem that Izzy's death arose from a sore ego, and in its rashness the killing went against the desires of Chicago.

And this wouldn't be the last time that an insult was reported as the reason Balistrieri had someone murdered. Of course, the truth was probably more a combination: Balistrieri wanted something from the victim (their possessions or their silence) and an insult or rude behaviour was the last straw – the thing that turned a want into a plan of action.

Here we find confusion in the research I was doing for this chapter. While my primary source is the FBI files and the investigations of these past agents, I strive to double check things whenever necessary and the date of the Frank's rise to power is thrown into some question here.

According to Wikipedia, Frank rose to power at a social event on December 27, 1961. This is attributed to AmericanMafia's Jay C. Ambler writing about the Milwaukee Mafia. However, this event doesn't show itself within the FBI's files and instead officers, agents, and informants all believe Balistrieri to be in charge by the end of 1960.

The informant that had first told agents that Balistrieri was now in charge returned on December 27 with a report on the hierarchy of Balistrieri's criminal family. August Maniaci was Balistrieri's first lieutenant and together with Balistrieri had assembled as their enforcers John Aiello, Buster Balistere and Steve Di Salvo.

This group made up what was known in the Milwaukee underworld as The Round Table. The Round Table was made up of *the* leaders of the Milwaukee underworld, the name being taken from the fact that they traditionally met at a round table in an establishment owned by whoever was the leader at the time.

Balistrieri's crew now sat The Round Table at his nightclub, Gallagher's.

On the same date, the Milwaukee Police Department told agents that there is little question that Balistrieri has definitely taken over leadership of the Italian-American hoodlum element from his father-in-law John Alioto.

It would seem then that Balistrieri was the boss by the time that 1961 came around.

And it would seem, he was not a welcome figure for the role.

On April 19, the FBI was informed that Balistrieri was feuding with the Chicago syndicate as headed up by Tony Accardo. The quarrel traces its origin to the Pogrob killing the previous year. Chicago did not approve the slaying of Pogrob. As a result of the killing, Chicago was claimed as thinking, there was an increase in police vigilance. According to informants, the Chicago syndicate was finding it difficult to continue earning money in light of this vigilance and so blamed Balistrieri.

The same informant went on to mention that Balistrieri has been able to keep his life, so far, because of his connections to Big Jim Balistrieri over in Kansas and because someone whose name is redacted in the files apparently was talking Chicago out of putting a hit on

Balistrieri. While the files do not give evidence as to who this person was, this story shows that Balistrieri was leaning on his uncle for support – was this what Buster and Di Salvo's 1960 trip to Kansas City ensured?

Some interesting events occur which the FBI, and informants, don't dwell on very much. One of particular interest was related to agents on April 25, 1961. According to the informant, about a month before there had been a pretty big robbery. The victim was one Tom Machi, who was reported as running a hangout for sexual perverts. Machi was a known gambler, suggesting that the robbery was over owed money. Milwaukee Phil, who was in reality working for Chicago, came to Milwaukee to see who fingered the robbery. The informant advised that while the robbery was likely done by Chicagoians, if it was fingered by someone from Milwaukee than Balistrieri or The Round Table would know who did it.

Also of interest is the fact that as he stepped into power, Balistrieri set forth an agenda to corrupt more political and police figures. FBI was put onto this by an informant in April. The goal was to get police department members, of any level, city councillors and members of the office of the District Attorney into compromising positions so as to have some dirt on them for blackmail. Put someone in a tricky enough situation and the blackmailing comes easily.

In regards to this plan, the FBI alerted the Milwaukee Police Department and a young detective would later lay out how Balistrieri tried to corrupt him through offers of free women, booze and merchandize.

On July 7, Balistrieri was placed on the FBI's list of hoodlums and racketeers selected for early prosecution. This would intensify the investigative efforts of the Milwaukee agents.

But only for a short time.

In the week that followed, it would seem that Balistrieri may have been prematurely selected: informants were now telling agents that Balistrieri, sometime in the near future, would be replaced as the nominal leader of the Italian-American syndicate in Milwaukee. He would be replaced because, according to one informant, Balistrieri had done nothing for anyone in the city and he had, because of the multitude of issues he had been facing with his clubs and taverns, gotten a lot of bad publicity.

Bad publicity, as it were, was a deadlier crime in the underworld than the murder of Izzy Pogrob had proved to be. Izzy Pogrob's death had shook the boat, where power within the Milwaukee Mafia was concerned.

Pogrob's death had gotten Chicago pissed at Balistrieri.

But Pogrob's death ultimately meant nothing.

Balistrieri still came to power, even in that fall out.

But bad publicity, that was something the organization was afraid of. We know that they took membership and a clean record very serious; Balistrieri would not have been allowed into the organization proper, in a position of policy and power, if he had had a criminal record. While bad publicity was not a criminal record, it brought attention.

Truly, when it comes to crime, any publicity is bad publicity.

And this is where the FBI and Balistrieri begin to part ways in the 1960s. The FBI continued to follow him, throughout 1961, but failed to reveal any solid evidence. Balistrieri would have a series of legal battles ahead of him in these years, from his use of B-girls to his taxes, which eventually would see him in jail.

The FBI's surveillance was still going as they entered 1961 but the file was closed soon afterwards. Between Vietnam, the counterculture and the social rights movement, the FBI's manpower ended up pointed in other directions and Balistrieri, once again, was deemed not to be important enough.

Four

The files of the FBI jump forward twelve years to 1973 to what might be the oddest moment of Frank's story. Indeed, it is barely even about Frank; he is a minor player in the perverse Shakespeanian drama that was the death of Sam Cesario. Sam's death, perhaps more than any of the multitude of murders that seemed to orbit around Balistrieri, highlights the absolute absurdity of violence within the organization.

First things first, the FBI file opens in 1973 and lists Frank Balistrieri, Charles Vince and Joseph Ferriola as the subjects under investigation. An unnamed individual provided information to the Bureau of Narcotics and Dangerous Drugs in Milwaukee that the three listed above had been involved in a conspiracy to murder Sam Cesario, who later wound up dead. The FBI knows that the three characters listed above were all inmates at the Federal Correctional Institute in Sandstone, Minnesota. Beyond that, the files go nowhere.

So let's break away from the FBI's files for a moment and see if we can answer some questions on our own. Who was Charles Vince and Joseph Ferriola? Who was Sam Cesario? And why did someone involved in the mafia in or around the Milwaukee area want him dead? And just how did he die anyway?

Let's start with that last question and go one better: not only do we know how he died, we know who killed him. We turn now to information gathered by Maurice Possley of the Chicago Tribune for his May 10, 1998, article entitled "The Organization Man." The article tracks the story of Harry

Aleman, nicknamed The Hook, who Possley refers to as

"argurably Chicago's most infamous murderer for hire."

Believed responsible for at least 18 mob murders between

1971 and 1977, Aleman began his career as a hitman with

the murder of his uncle: Sam "Sambo" Cesario. Harry

Aleman and another man, suspected of being his friend

William "Butch" Petrocelli, adorned skimasks and

approached Cesario while he sat in a chair on his front lawn

with his wife.

Cesario was smoking a cigar when the men approached.

They beat him to death with clubs, shooting him to be sure

that he was dead.

Cesario had been a member of the Chicago Outfit, a

known bookmaker working out of Cicero, Illinois. The

nclusion of this factoid here would seem to plant the idea

hat Cesario's death was a typical mod hit – he didn't earn

enough, was skimming too much, bringing too much heat, or just pissing off the wrong person. But there is nothing typical about the death of Cesario – no, there's nothing normal in being killed by a ghost.

See, Cesario had made an enemy. One that he didn't know he even had. One whose power could bring violence from beyond the grave. In the world of organized crime, the body may die but violence … violence is immortal.

So how did Cesario come to piss off a ghost? Did he perhaps rob a tomb? Maybe provoke an ancient family curse? No, of course not. Cesario was a part of reality, so it began as any good tale of crime and murder begins: with a woman.

This one's name was Nancy and she seems as much a victim in this story as Cesario.

Gerry DeNono, a low level mobster with a connection to the Chicago Outfit and a history of burgalry and murder who went government witness, told the story of what happened to Cesario on camera.

Turns out, Cesario got on the wrong side of Milwaukee Phil.

"Nancy came over to me," Gerry tells in his own words, 'and she said, "Listen, Gerry, do me a favour. Take me to Cesario's tonight. After you finish eating.' She left the table and Joe said to me, 'You don't drive her nowhere, you don't talk to her no more, you stay away from her.'"

"I say, 'I ain't doing nothing, I ain't fooling around with her.'

"He said, 'No, I'm not saying you're fooling around. Don't go near her.'"

"I says, 'Why?'"

"He says, 'That's Milwaukee Phil's girlfriend.'"

"He was in the federal penitentiary at the time. But that was still his girlfriend, even though he was married. Now he's married, got kids, but that's his girlfriend and you're not supposed to talk to his girlfriend."

"I laugh, says, 'Okay.'"

"Months later, she was dating this guy's name is Blackie [Sam Cesario], he was a bookmaker in Cicero. And Nan went to ask Milwaukee Phil for permission to get married to Blackie. And … He's married now, you get this? He's in prison, he gives his permission to her to marry this other guy, this other mustache, alright?"

"He dies. He dies in prison. Joe tells me, he says, 'You see Blackie over there? He's dead.'"

"I say, 'What for? Milwaukee Phil's dead? He died in prison, and that's only his girlfriend Joe, what the hell's the difference?'"

"He said, 'From his grave, he ordered the hit.'"

"Three weeks later, after they were married, Blackie was shot right in front of Nan in a rocking chair at the house."

"From the grave he ordered that hit."

"Just told me, don't be fooling around with no one else's girlfriend, that's all. It just showed me that this man had so much power, so much control over people, that outta respect they killed this guy because of Blackie dating Milwaukee Phil's girlfriend. Which don't make any sense to me but I'm just saying this is their mind, this goes to show you how their mind thinks."

The minds of the men that made up these syndicates were violent beyond belief. But despite the fact that a ghost ordered the hit, it was still up to the living to put it into motion.

In that respect, we return to the names Frank Balistrieri, Charles Vince and Joseph Ferriola. Balistrieri we know, but who are the other two?

Charles Vince was suspected of being underboss to Joseph Zammuto, the head of the Rockford crime family from 1958 to 1973. Charles Vince then represents a member out one of the syndicates active in New York state.

Ferriola would pass away in 1989, having helped run the Chicago Outfit from 1985 to 1988. At this moment in time Ferriola was working for Joey Aiuppa, who was leader in Chicago from 1971 until he fell in the casino skim that will shortly take Balistrieri down.

Together, Balistrieri, Ferriola and Vince represented three different crime families, all suspected by the FBI of being involved in the conspiracy to kill Cesario.

Milwaukee Phil may have ordered the hit, but being dead, it was up to these three to figure out who to call to get it done. From within the prison, a hit passed from one member to three others, who then brought it into reality. Out of respect? What respect is there in the act? Did those involved really believe that they were in some way, any way, committing an honorable act?

And what of the living? The poor widow who had explicitly taken it upon herself to seek out Milwaukee Phil's permission? What becomes of his lie to her that it was alright?

If there was any sort of honor in the murder itself, that guise is torn away when one considers the absolute disgusting setup.

But in their world, things worked differently.

Violence was merely just one tool in their kit. Violence was a message. Violence was a means.

And violence was so prominent that it failed to register as violence at it.

It was merely business as usual.

Five

At this point, it's important to understand just how poorly the FBI's files reflect the actions of Balistrieri at this time. The information relating to Balistrieri's involvement in the casino skim, our main area of focus this chapter, is rather minimal. Likely, this is caused by two reasons.

The first reason is that Balistrieri was far from the only hoodlum involved in the skim. This would mean that in order to properly track the FBI's following of the casino skimming we would need to put in FOI requests for all the possibly people involved. And, by the time the skim came collapsing, we know at least 15 people that had charges brought against them for their involvement. This means that massive amount of information would be required from the

FBI. And, frankly, that is not what the focus of this book is. We're following Balistrieri's life here.

The second reason is that the FBI had clearly had issues in penetrating the Vegas casinos that were involved in skimming. We know that in 1963, the FBI released a two volume document called *The Skimming Report* to the Department of Justice. However, the information inside of the report was obtained through illegal surveillance and so they were unable to bring any charges down at the time. That the only way the FBI could find out about skimming was through illegal surveillance helps to enlighten us on just how hard it was to penetrate these operations.

Before we continue into a look at the skim in micro, let's first set up the macro view. The casino skim was a criminal activity undertaken by Kansas City and Milwaukee's syndicates, with the Chicago Outfit coming in at a later point for arbitration. The syndicates used a company called the Argent Corporation, which was run by a man by the name of Allen R. Glick. In 1974, Argent would purchase the Hacienda Casino and acquire a gaming licence. Argent would then go on to purchase the Recrion Corporation, which owned the Stardust and Fremont casinos. A number of deaths were to pop up related to Argent, which is no surprise as Argent was syphoning, or skimming, money from the casinos – where there is money, there is a crime and where there is crime, there is violence. Argent, and the syndicates involved therein, would be forced out of the casino business in the late '70s and eventually the syndicates (but not Glick) would be called to face the law for their participation in skim.

So let us look to the questions this raises: Who was Glick? Why didn't he do any jail time? How was Argent able to afford a casino? How exactly does a casino skim work? Why did Chicago get brought in to arbitrate and what did they take in return? And what about those murders?

Balistrieri will make an appearance early in this story and then begin to fade away. But realize that his role is foundational, it puts him as one of the key players despite so much seeming to happen beyond him.

In March of 1974, Balistrieri travelled to Los Vegas. There he met up with Kansas City hoodlums Carl DeLuna and Nicholas Civella. Civella was the boss of Kansas City for about thirty years by the time of his death in 1983. At some point during this meeting, the Kansas City gangsters arranged for Balistrieri to meet Allen Glick. The meeting was to be a fortuitous one for Balistrieri and the Kansas syndicate.

For a time.

Balistrieri would later go on to say that he had an obligation to Glick. That obligation would be helping him to acquire a $62 million dollar loan from the Teamsters Union. Exactly what was that obligation? Likely, it wasn't any such thing but a desire to partake in the spoils that came from the casino skim: money, and lots and lots of it at that.

But who was Glick?

Glick was a front-man for the mob's move into casinos. It turned out, as Glick regrettable found, that he was a nobody, truly. He had no power, he was in control in name only. Glick was someone with a clean record, exactly the kind of person the syndicates needed if they were to get licencing to run a casino.

And so, Balistrieri helped Glick acquire funding through the teamster's loan. This allowed Glick to purchase the Hacienda in 1974 and acquire a Nevada gaming licence. To purchase the casino, Glick used his company, Argent. It was taken from the first letter from each of his names, Allen R. Glick, and the first three letters of enterprises.

Glick followed the purchase of the Hacienda by also purchasing the Stardust and the Fremont. Together, these three casinos represented a massive investment on the part of Milwaukee and Kansas City's Italian-American organizations. In the time that the casino skim was active, Argent Corporation's casinos were suspected of syphoning off between $7 and $15 million dollars in funds.

And the best part? It was entirely untraceable.

Perhaps the best explanation for how a casino skim works is in 1995's *Casino*. Truly, it takes you inside to show you how the sausage is made, as it were. But the core concept is very easy to grasp and deviously simple.

A lot of money passes through a casino. An absolute shit-ton, to put it bluntly. So much so, that counting the money a casino makes is a full time, around the clock job. The thing with all that money is that the more there is, the easier it is for some of it to get lost. Think about walking around the streets of New York City or Toronto or Tokyo; there are so many people, that one becomes lost in the crowd. In a casino, there is so much money that if some were to disappear out the back before it happened to have been counted … Well, who's to say it was even there in the first place?

The beauty in a casino skim is that it hides in plain sight.

Because the money would be taken before being logged into the casino's corporate accounts, it meant it was untaxed. Every dollar stollen was a dollar full.

But with that much money now moving from Vegas back East to Milwaukee and Kansas, the greed that drives the criminal underworld began to rear its head. True, it was never far to begin with, the very fact that they put the skim in place shows as much, but with that much money coming home things began to get heated.

The Hacienda was purchased in 1974, by 1976 it was being said that Balistrieri and Civella were quarrelling over the division of the funds. What started the quarrell seems to have been lost to time but the two men seem to have found a fair solution. Instead of dragging either of the families into an unneeded war, for which the Cleveland organization was being looked down upon at that time, the men decided to approach Chicago for arbitration in the matter.

It doesn't seem either man was satisfied as this brought Chicago in for 25% of the earnings. But it did prevent a war.

It also introduced Frank Rosenthal into the story, the character of which Robert De Niro played a fictionalized version of in *Casino*.

Rosenthal was sent by Chicago to oversee what was happening in Vegas. He had worked in sports gambling and transitioned over when Chicago became involved. Rosenthal had a helluva time. He couldn't get proper licencing because of a criminal record, so he secretly ran the casinos for Argent while switching from job to job, whatever positions the casinos had that didn't require him to be licenced.

In 1982, after everything had begun to go to hell, Rosenthal would come face to face with Balistrieri's violence – he was called the Mad Bomber, after all.

But before we turn to that, let's take a brief look at how Argent Corp seemed no stranger to violence, either.

We turn our attention to the murders of Tamara Rand and Edward Buccieri.

Glick received a loan from the Teamsters Union in order to fund the purchase of the Hacienda. Balistrieri helped Glick to get this particular loan. However, Tamara Rand (according to KLAS-TV and KIQY radio) had helped Glick to fund Argent's purchase of Recrion Corporation. Recrion controlled the Stardust and Fremont casinos. This means that the purchase of Recrion Corporation gave Argent three casinos, instead of one, thus more than doubling the amount that the syndicates could expect to generate.

Rand, according to the above mentioned sources, had helped Glick to fund the purchase of Recrion through a loan of $500,000. According to Rand, this entitled her to a 5% ownership share in Argent. Of course, it's never a very good idea to tell the mafia what it is that they owe you.

And so, to little surprise for those following along, Tamara Rand was found dead in her San Francisco home on November 9, 1975. Rand had been shot five times by a .22 caliber gun with a silencer attached.

Rand's wasn't the first death, however.

Earlier in the year, May, saw the murder of Edward Buccieri. Buccieri had been a pit boss at Caesar's Palace, another Vegas casino. He also was a distant relative of Chicago underboss Fiori "Fifi" Buccieri and had an astounding number of connections within the Vegas underworld.

And he used those connections to help Glick to get the Teamster's Loan in the first place.

Glick, remember, very quickly learned that he had no power over his own casinos. He was told, explicitly, that he owed the mafia money for their hand in helping him acquire the loan.

And they told him to stay the hell out of Rosenthal's way.

So when Buccieri came calling in 1975, to inform Glick that the powerless man now also owed Buccieri $30,000 as a finders fee for his help setting up the loan … Well, Glick just wasn't the person to be bothered about it.

And so, Glick did the reasonable thing. He told Rosenthal about Buccieri's demands.

Within a couple days Buccieri was dead, shot in the head with a .25 caliber round while he sat in his car.

Argent, it would seem, had a protector. Not out of loyalty to Glick, however, but a protector none-the-less.

At least, it seemed that way.

On October 4, 1982, Frank Rosenthal left Tony Roma's restaurant at 602 East Sahara Ave, Los Vegas, and proceeded to his car. Rosenthal opened the door to the 1981 Cadillac Eldorado and shuffled inside, his thin form barely filling out the driver's seat.

He put the key into the ignition and watched as hell split open around him.

Attached to the gas tank had been a bomb, set to explode when the engine attempted to turn over. And, in that regard, the bomb did exactly as expected.

The car exploded around Rosenthal, who, against every odd, was able to tumble from the vehicle, rolling on the ground to put out the fire that was eating away at his clothing.

Rosenthal only survived because of a chance of fate. The Cadillac Eldorado was an interesting car. See, during the manufacturing process, Cadillac came up against a problem in the design. The car had balancing issues. So, in order to work around those issues, Cadillac installed a thick metal plate under the driver's seat.

What Rosenthal, Cadillac or the people who set the bomb couldn't have predicted was that the metal plate under the driver's side would prevent the worst of the blast from blowing Rosenthal to bits. Instead, it acted as a shield and it saved Rosenthal's life.

It was clear that things were going to shit in regards to the casino; Glick's guardian angel wasn't even safe. And, when the rumors of who was responsible came down the line, was it any surprise that Glick went state's witness?

Wouldn't you, if you heard that Frank "The Mad Bomber" Balistrieri was looking to silence the parties involved, like he tried to silence Rosenthal?

<u>Six</u>

On the morning of September 11, 1975, August J. Maniaci was shot to death while sitting at the wheel of his car, parked behind his house while preparing to leave for work. Though the murder didn't go unnoticed, and has remained unsolved despite the finding of the murder weapon, it wasn't of enough interest to the FBI to begin a file on it quite yet. It is of great interest to us however, as it was said that August and his brother Vincent had been battling with Balistrieri.

That is, to be clear, it wasn't of interest to the FBI until 1977 when a new file was opened. The targets of this file were Frank Balistrieri, Peter Balistrieri, and Steve Di Salvo. The crime in question? The FBI has it listed as: August S.

Maniaci - Victim; Vincent J. Maniaci - Victim. The title would later be changed to correct August's middle initial.

At various times throughout this story, we have seen August Maniaci's name pop up. When Balistrieri was first coming into power, we saw that he was among the list of people which Balistrieri was unpopular with. However, we later saw his name come up again: this time as one of Balistrieri's underlings. Tracing the history of lower level figures throughout their criminal careers, particularly how their feelings towards those around them (and the feelings people had on them) are nearly impossible. However, rumors of the Maniaci brothers's feuding with Balistrieri filtered through the grapevine and it had been suggested that August was an FBI informant. He was known to get into shouting matches with Di Salvo and Balistrieri was of the mind that he had to kill August before August killed him.

Regardless of our ability to trace the exact issue that causes Balistrieri to order his death, we can see that August was in fact killed. So, too, could his brother Vincent who was to be released from federal detention in June of 1977. Fearing reprisals for the killing of his brother, Balistrieri ordered Vincent killed in the way that made the most sense considering his history: a car bombing.

August 17, 1977, Vincent Maniaci was having car troubles. He wasn't sure what the issue was, though, so he took it into the garage. Diving under the hood, mechanics were shocked to find out what looked like an explosive had been attached to the engine block. Clearly in over their heads, the garage telephoned the police who came to handle the situation.

Police removed a dynamite bomb from under the hood. Composed of 20 sticks of Red Arrow 70%, and a pound of booster, the TNT explosive was supposed to trigger when Vincent turned the key and started the ignition. The alligator clips that were to serve as leads were improperly connected to the engine block and frame and thus failed to trigger detonation upon turning over.

Vincent was lucky.

He knew it and so did the entire criminal underworld and so did FBI. They state clearly in their files, though never point out where the knowledge came from, that it was a known fact that a contract had been put out on Vicent Maniaci's head. The reason was as old as violence: hurt my enemy before they can hurt me. Balistrieri killed his brother, so Vincent had ample cause for revenge.

But it never came to pass.

Having heard about the contract before the failed car bombing had even taken place, the FBI had already begun trying to pinpoint where the Balistrieri crew was meeting to discuss the planned killing. Di Salvo is singled out here as their primary surveillance target, which is an important fact to keep note of. They observed Di Salvo meeting several groups of underworld figures but none that pointed towards Maniaci in anyway.

And so, on August 11, the FBI wrote that Balistrieri had called off the hit on Maniaci.

Six days later he was in the garage having a bomb removed from his car.

The FBI clearly had a hard time handling the Balistrieri organization. But despite their struggles, they kept after him.

Vincent Maniaci, on the other hand, knew a miracle when he saw one and left Balistrieri the hell alone. Maniaci would live another five years, almost to the day, longer than Balistrieri did.

In the middle of their investigation into August's death, which was to continue well into the 1980s when Balistrieri was already behind bars, the FBI released a notice in The New York Times under the title "Crime Leaders as Cited by F.B.I." The August 6, 1978, article was a single paragraph followed by a list of cities/states and names. Reading down the lengthy list of figures, you come to "Milwaukee – Frank Balistrieri."

And so, in a single line, the FBI told the world who Frank was.

At this time, Balistrieri had more issues than a man ever should. The local police were continuing to put pressure onto his gambling operations. The FBI was investigating him in relation to the casino skim, the Maniaci attempted/homicide, as well as Balistrieri's corruption of government officials within and around Milwaukee.

While the FBI's files are quite boring in these regards, quite often showing more redactions than information, one of the most baffling and most intriguing comes from their continued (and ultimately fruitless) efforts to bring the Maniaci homicide to justice.

A letter dated 5/7/79 from the Milwaukee branch to the home office of the FBI reads as follows: "As of this date the United States Department of Justice has not formally notified the United States Attorney's (USA) Office, Milwaukee, Eastern District of Wisconsin (EDW), of its decision in regard to the revised immunity request for STEVE J. DI SALVO. The Department of Justice had previously refused to grant immunity to DI SALVO, but the request was re-submitted in an effort to bring the AUGUST J. MANIACI [sic] shooting and the VICENT J. MANIACI attempted bombing before the Federal Grand Jury (FGJ).

The opinion of the USA's Office … is that the Department will not grant the immunity where there is not a reasonable chance of the individual (DI SALVO) testifying before the FGJ and in the alternative be incarcerated."

Here was the real bomb in the Maniaci situation: Why was Milwaukee trying to gain immunity for Di Salvo? It seems unlikely that they would first seek to get immunity before approaching the man to gauge his interest or the chance that he would become an informant. Did the FBI approach Di Salvo to become an informant and he refused unless he received immunity? This is one way the information can be read. The USA's Office did not think there was a good enough chance that Di Salvo would take the stand to testify. This would point that he was not offering to be witness but rather to inform. This reading points towards Di Salvo's loyalty.

Other options point towards Di Salvo already working with the FBI but unable to get protection from a murder charge. Seeing how many figures in the underworld are known to have played both sides so as to soften the impact of the charges brought against them if they were ever caught, this reading isn't entirely without merit.

But whether or not Di Salvo was a rat is less important than the bigger picture this document points to. If they were looking for immunity for figures as close to Balistrieri as Di Salvo was, then who else could they have been speaking with? As we push into these later years, more and more information is redacted from the files … what other names might be hidden beneath the blacked out text in these files?

<u>End</u>

August S. Palmisano woke up early on the morning of June 30, 1978. Palmisano, a known gambler who the police were watching, would have been nervous but the man had a mean streak that wouldn't quit. He was known to get into fights with Balistrieri, saying things to his face that no man should be able to say. But Palmisano said them anyway, couldn't help it, he wasn't afraid of Balistrieri.

More troubling was the police. It had only just come out in the papers the month before that the FBI was tapping his phone. Balistrieri's too. That put Balistrieri and Palmisano together in the FBI's mind and that wasn't a good thing. Palmisano didn't want to go down for Balistrieri's crimes. Not after what he tried to do to Vincent, a good friend of his.

No, as Palmisano travelled down to the underground parking lot where he kept his car, his mind wasn't on Balistrieri but how the hell he was going to get out in front of this investigation and redirect the heat towards the Milwaukee Don.

Palmisano got into his car shortly before nine o'clock that morning and started the engine.

Residents of the apartment building on the third floor reported that they thought an earthquake had hit. Pictures were knocked off the walls as the building shook.

Palmisano had turned the key in the ignition and sparked he triggering mechanism on the bomb that had been wired under the hood while he had slept upstairs. The explosion ore the front of the car apart. The seat Palmisano was sitting n was hurled into the back of the car, parts of the man's body shooting out across the garage while the flames cooked what stayed sitting.

While Palmisano slept, Balistrieri showed himself to be a step ahead of the man. Shortly afterwards, Balistrieri was quoted as saying "He called me a name – to my face – and now they can't find his skin!"

It is doubtful that the murder was purely to heal Balistrieri's damaged ego. Palmisano had done two years of probation on gambling charges in the past and Balistrieri likely suspected the man to be cooperating with the authorities.

Gambling was to prove Balistrieri's Achilles heel regardless.

Despite the fact that it had never ceased to cause trouble and be a pain in the ass, Balistrieri continued to keep a tight fist on gambling operations.

And the city of Milwaukee knew it.

In 1983, at the age of 65, Frank Balistrieri was convicted of five gambling and tax charges. May 30, 1984, Balistrieri was sentenced to 13 years in prison.

While serving his term, the casino skim came crumbling down. And so in September of 1985, Balistrieri was one of many high level Mafia members tried for stealing roughly $2 million dollars of illegal income through their connection to Argent Corporation.

Balistrieri plead guilty.

Meanwhile, new proceedings against Balistrieri came out of Kansas and he also ended up pleading guilty to conspiracy and racketeering.

What began with gambling ended with Balistrieri looking at the rest of his years in prison though he was spared that fate.

He was released early on November 5th, 1991, due to poor health and the longest running, in many regards the last great, father of the Milwaukee Mafia passed away due to natural causes on February 7, 1993.

Cast of Characters

Tony Accardo: Born 1906, Tony Accardo served as boss of the Chicago Outfit from 1947 to 195 7 when he stepped down from acting boss. He continued to be an important figure in the syndicate, controlling decisions from the shadows.

Felix "Milwaukee Phil" Alderisio: A prominent member of the Chicago Outfit, Milwaukee Phil worked many different jobs in the criminal underworld. Though he would eventually die in prison, Milwaukee Phil would be responsible for a murder – that happened after he was dead.

John Alioto: Alioto was acting boss of the Milwaukee organization from 1952–1961. Frank Balistrieri married Alioto's daughter, making Alioto his father-in-law.

Buster Balestrere: Cousin of Frank Balistrieri, Buster came to Milwaukee from Kansas and would serve as Frank's muscle.

"Big Jim" Balistrieri: Uncle of Frank, Big Jim was a powerful figure in the Kansas organization, through which Frank was able to find backing and support.

Frank Balistrieri: The last, most power Godfather of the Milwaukee Mafia and the subject of this book.

Joseph Balistrieri: Frank and Peter Balistrieri's father, the FBI files point towards the sons taking after their old man

Peter Balistrieri: Brother of Frank Balistrieri, the subject of this book, Peter was an ally of his brother's whose named was used to allow Frank to run more taverns than the city allowed..

Walter "Blackie" Brocca: A member of the Milwaukee underworld, Blackie at various times worked as a wheelman for Balistrieri and was said to be at war with Balistrieri, having picked sides with Phil Valley.

Edward Buccieri: Buccieri was a pitboss at Caesar's Palace casino in Las Vegas. His ties to Argent Corporation and the casino skimming operation lead to his murder in 1975.

Marshall Caifano: A member of the Chicago Outfit, Caifano played a big role in Los Vegas' criminal underground during the 1950s.

Sam Cesario: Cesario was a member of the Chicago outfit that was murdered in 1971 for getting married to Milwaukee Phil's girlfriend.

Nicholas Civella: Civella ran the Kansas City syndicate and was greatly involved in everything from the gambling and the casino skimming to the assassination of Leon Jordan.

Carl DeLuna: Second in command to Kansas City's boos Nicholas Civella. DeLuna's home would eventually be raided in regards to the casino skim and it would be found that DeLuna kept extensive notes which allowed the government to proceed with criminal charges.

Sam Ferrara: Ferrara was the leader of Milwaukee syndicate from 1949 until 1952, at which point John Alioto took over as boss. Ferrara was considered to be inactive within Milwaukee's criminal underworld by 1963.

Joseph Ferriola: Head of the Chicago Outfit from 1986 to 1989, Ferriola would go to prison for his part in the casino skim.

Allen R. Glick: Glick was the owner of Argent Corporation, the company through which Milwaukee and Kansas City's syndicates were able to begin skimming Las Vegas casinos. Glick would turn state's witness as everything was going to hell.:

August Maniaci: Having been a thorn in Balistrieri's side for some time, August was killed and his brother Vicent was targeted for death but survived through luck.

Vincent Maniaci: Brother of the murdered August Maniaci. The Maniaci brothers were thought to be at war with Balistrieri. After August's death, Vincent was lucky to survive a poorly wired car bombing attempt.

August S. Palmisano: In the weeks following his death by car bombing, Palmisano had gotten into several heated and public arguments with Balistrieri. After his death, Balistrieri was quoted as saying, "He called me a name – to my face – and now they can't find his skin!"

Izzy Pogrob: The owner of a local club, it is believed that Balistrieri had Pogrob killed. However, Chicago was not happy to find out that Pogrob had been murdered and so was "down on Balistrieri."

John Polcyn: Chief of Milwaukee police from 1945 until 1957, Polcyn was rumored to have been a friend of, or at least blackmailed by, Balistrieri.

Tamara Rand: Rand lent $500,000 to Allen R. Glick to help Argent Corporation purchase more casinos. For payment, she was murdered on November 9, 1975.

Johnny Rizzo: A known gambler, Rizzo helped run Balistrieri's gambling operations in Kenosha during the 1960s.

Frank "Lefty" Rosenthal: A member of the Chicago Outfit, Rosenthal was in charge of running the Argent Corporation's casinos. He was nearly killed in a car bombing thought to be Balistrieri's doing.

Steve Di Salvo: One of Balistrieri's muscle men, Di Salvo worked Frank for many years, often alongside Buster.

Frank Stelloh: A close associate of Balistrieri's organization, Stelloh was suspected as having been involved in the Izzy Pogrob murder.

John Di Trapani: A member of the Milwaukee organization, Trapani was killed in the 1950s on the order of Milwaukee Phil.

Phil Valley: A member of Milwaukee's criminal underground, Valley at times was Balistrieri's friend and his enemy. Valley also held power within Milwaukee's Cooks, Waiters and Bartenders Union.

Charles Vince: Vince was underboss to Rockford crime family leader Joseph Zammuto.

For Further Study

Leaving Los Vegas by Gary Jenkins (Please buy via his web page to support his Gangland Wire Podcast, https://ganglandwire.com)

Milwaukee Mafia by Gavid Schmit

Straw Men by Magnesen

Wayne Clingman's documentary, *Milwaukee Mafia - Frank Balistrieri* can be found at https://amazon.com/gp/video/detail/B07Mc98R8Z/ref=pd_c bc_318_5

About the Authors

Wayne Clingman is a long time fan of history, both the kind they teach in school and the history "they" want kept hidden. Wayne lives in a 115 year old home in Racine, Wisconsin, with his wife, Barb, four Alasken malamutes, and a cat that controls his life. Wayne is the producer of *Milwaukee Mafia - Frank Balistrieri*. This is his first book.

Zack Long is a novelist, screenwriter, film director, webmaster, editor,film historian, and master of horror. He is the editor-in-chief and creative mind behind Scriptophobic.ca, a site dedicated to helping genre screen/writers; the author of *Scream Writing: A Comprehensive Guide to Writing the Horror Screenplay*, and has had his writings published in Grim Magazine, Film and Fishnets, and on sites across the web.